How to Use This Book

Planning meals can be a real struggle, day after day. Now there's help! This book offers a method that will help you become better organized in your efforts to plan tasty, homecooked meals for your family and friends.

WELCOME TO MY KITCHEN is a write-your-own menu organizer, attractively illustrated and arranged by season for easy reference.

You'll notice that this book is in five sections – each a different color. This was done to divide our meals into the four seasons of the year plus an extra section for special occasions or mood meals we all have.

Use the blue pages to record memorable winter meals, the peach pages for springtime spreads, the yellow ones for summer menus, and the tan ones for fall favorites. The white pages are for those special meals you remember from childhood and menus that don't fit into a season.

I have included a few sample menus we love at our house, just to get you started. Once you have filled in your own menu ideas, your meal plans will be ready and waiting. Think how handy that will be on all those days when you feel uninspired about what to fix for dinner!

In addition to recording family favorites, there's plenty of space to include menus for:

- Entertaining and planning for a crowd
- Holiday get-togethers
- Special celebrations such as birthdays and family reunions
- Meals you've enjoyed in restaurants and would like to duplicate at home
- Meals that go together quickly for those days you don't have much time

- *Meals that are low in calories*
- *Meals that use leftovers*

Your personal organizer will also help keep track of everybody's favorite dishes. And because WELCOME TO MY KITCHEN is organized according to the seasons, you'll be reminded to take advantage of the fresh produce and special foods which are best at certain times of the year.

I've found that by using this planner, grocery shopping has been easier and I'm spending less, because I know exactly what main dishes and side dishes I'm planning to serve.

HINT: Because you're the author of this book you'll want to put your name on the cover and the title page. I suggest using permanent ink such as those made by Windsor-Newton. The permanent felt-tip markers are not recommended because they tend to "fuzz" and look messy. I do encourage you to cover the front and back of your book with clear contact paper to protect it from kitchen spills.

It is my hope that this book will help you be creative with your meals, to be an organized and relaxed hostess, and happy to welcome loved ones into your kitchen.

ABOUT THE ILLUSTRATOR/PUBLISHER

Nancy Radcliffe Edwards has been drawing and painting since childhood. She graduated from the University of Mississippi, owned an art gallery in Houston, Texas, and was a founder of the Houston Watercolor Society. Her portraits and watercolors have been purchased for many collections and reproductions. In 1977 she was named an Outstanding Young Woman of America. She is the illustrator/publisher of the book WITH LOVE FROM MY KITCHEN a best-selling recipe organizer published in 1984. Wife and mother of two teenagers, Nancy lives in Minnesota.

Index for Special Menus

Index

Tempura
*once a year meal

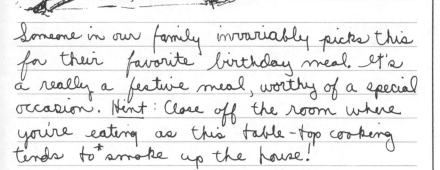

Someone in our family invariably picks this
for their favorite birthday meal. It's
a really a festive meal, worthy of a special
occasion. Hint: Close off the room where
you're eating as this table-top cooking
tends to *smoke up the house!

Place your wok or elec. frying pan in the
center of the table where all can reach.
    Hot oil in wok - add salt to cut down
        on spattering - peanut oil recommended
    Fondue forks - to spear food + cook
    Foods to cook: chicken, shrimp, scallops
    onions (cut into rings), fresh spinach leaves,
    whole fresh mushrooms, green pepper, water
    chestnuts, & apple slices

Comments:
Selected food is dipped into a flour, egg,
milk batter + each is cooked in hot oil.
Serve rice and hot tea. You may
wish to add some hot mustard and
sweet + sour sauce for cooked foods.
    Truly a celebration meal!

Special Menus

Comments:

Comments:

Special Menus

Comments:

Special Menus

Comments:

Special Menus

Comments:

Special Menus

_____
_____
_____
_____
_____
_____
_____
_____
_____
_____
_____
_____
_____
_____
_____
_____

Comments:
_____
_____
_____
_____
_____
_____

Special Menus

Comments:

Special Menus

Comments:

Special Menus

Comments:

Comments:

Special Menus

Comments:

Comments:

Special Menus

_____
_____
_____
_____
_____
_____
_____
_____
_____
_____
_____
_____
_____
_____
_____
_____
_____
_____
_____

Comments:

_____
_____
_____
_____
_____
_____

Comments:

Special Menus

_____

_____

_____

_____

_____

_____

_____

_____

_____

_____

_____

_____

_____

Comments:

_____

_____

_____

_____

_____

_____

Special Menus

_____

_____

_____

_____

_____

_____

_____

_____

_____

_____

_____

_____

_____

_____

_____

_____

_____

_____

_____

_____

Comments:

_____

_____

_____

_____

_____

Special Menus

Comments:

Comments:

Special Menus

_____
_____
_____
_____
_____
_____
_____
_____
_____
_____
_____
_____
_____
_____
_____
_____

Comments:

_____
_____
_____
_____
_____
_____

Special Menus

Comments:

Special Menus

_____
_____
_____
_____
_____
_____
_____
_____
_____
_____
_____
_____
_____
_____
_____
_____
_____
_____

Comments:

_____
_____
_____
_____
_____
_____

Special Menus

Comments:

Special Menus

Comments:

Special Menus

Comments:

Special Menus

Comments:

Index for Winter Menus

Menu	Page

Index

Roast Beef — oven meal

Roast a large cut of beef in the oven

Make gravy from pan drippings

Potatoes — bake in oven, have grated cheese, chives, bacon bits, and sour cream to garnish at the table

Fresh broccoli — do at the last minute so it's not overcooked; the aroma can get overpowering.

Dessert — Apples baked with butter, cinnamon and brown sugar

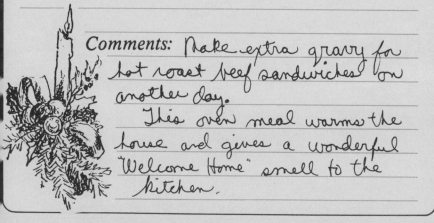

Comments: Make extra gravy for hot roast beef sandwiches on another day.

This oven meal warms the house and gives a wonderful "Welcome Home" smell to the kitchen.

Winter Menus

_____

_____

_____

_____

_____

_____

_____

_____

_____

_____

_____

_____

_____

_____

_____

Comments:

_____

_____

_____

_____

_____

Comments:

Winter Menus

Comments:

Winter Menus

_____
_____
_____
_____
_____
_____
_____
_____
_____
_____
_____
_____
_____
_____
_____
_____
_____
_____
_____
_____

Comments:

_____
_____
_____
_____
_____
_____

Winter Menus

_____
_____
_____
_____
_____
_____
_____
_____
_____
_____
_____
_____
_____
_____
_____

Comments:

_____
_____
_____
_____
_____

Winter Menus

Comments:

Winter Menus

_____

_____

_____

_____

_____

_____

_____

_____

_____

_____

_____

_____

_____

_____

_____

_____

Comments:

_____

_____

_____

_____

_____

_____

Winter Menus

Comments:

Winter Menus

Comments:

Winter Menus

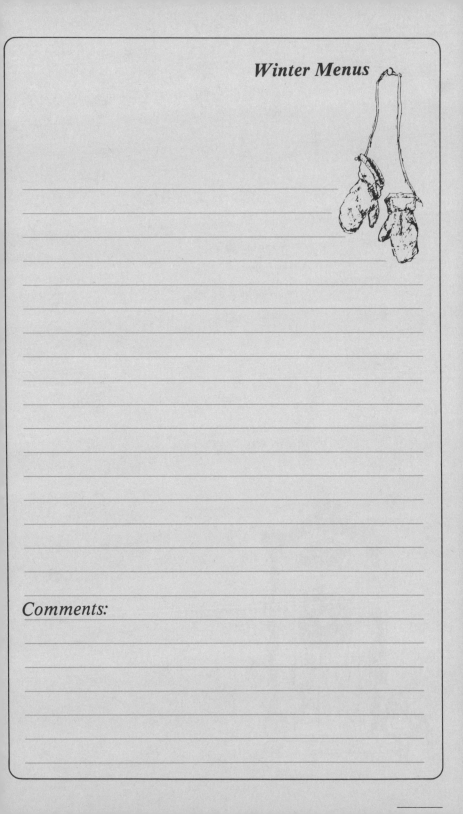

_____

_____

_____

_____

_____

_____

_____

_____

_____

_____

_____

_____

_____

_____

_____

_____

_____

Comments:

_____

_____

_____

_____

_____

Winter Menus

Comments:

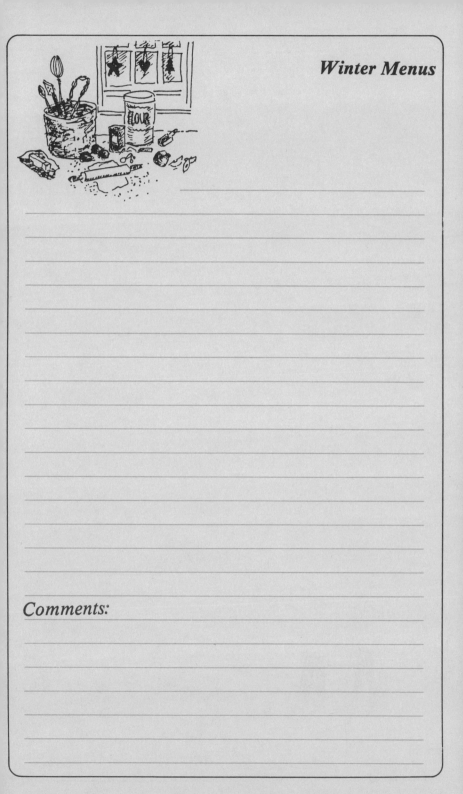

Winter Menus

Comments:

Winter Menus

Comments:

Winter Menus

Comments:

Winter Menus

Comments:

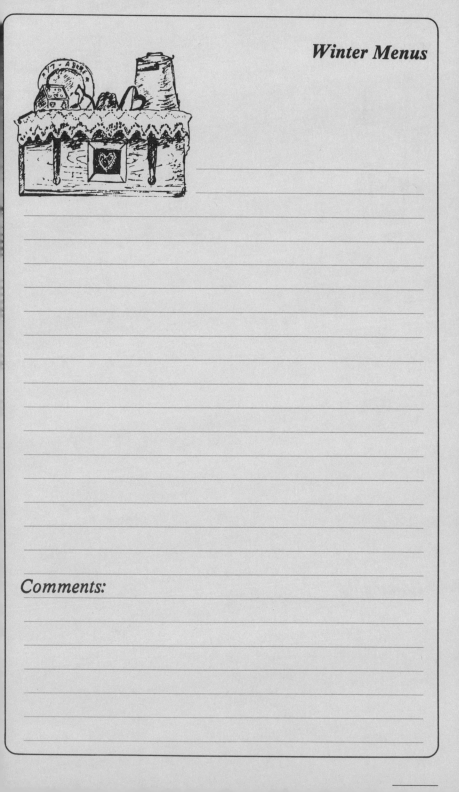

Comments:

Winter Menus

_____

_____

_____

_____

_____

_____

_____

_____

_____

_____

_____

_____

_____

_____

_____

_____

Comments:

_____

_____

_____

_____

_____

Winter Menus

Comments:

Winter Menus

_____
_____
_____
_____
_____
_____
_____
_____
_____
_____
_____
_____
_____
_____
_____
_____
_____
_____
_____

Comments:

_____
_____
_____
_____
_____

Winter Menus

Comments:

Winter Menus

Comments:

Winter Menus

_____
_____
_____
_____
_____
_____
_____
_____
_____
_____
_____
_____
_____
_____
_____
_____
_____
_____
_____
_____
_____
_____

Comments:

_____
_____
_____
_____
_____

Winter Menus

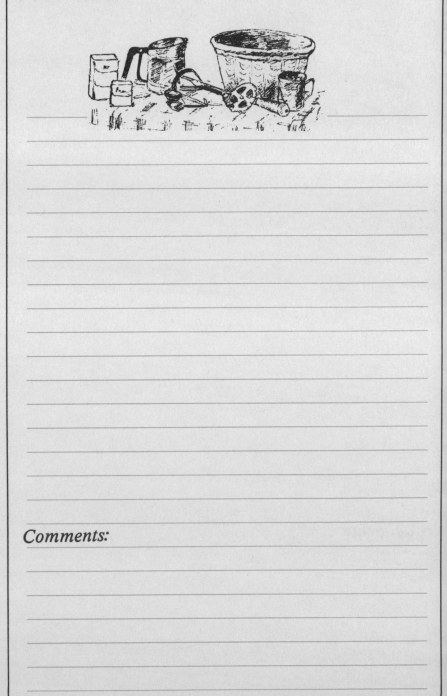

Comments:

Winter Menus

Comments:

Winter Menus

_____

_____

_____

_____

_____

_____

_____

_____

_____

_____

_____

_____

_____

_____

_____

_____

Comments:

_____

_____

_____

_____

_____

_____

Winter Menus

Comments:

Winter Menus

Comments:

Winter Menus

Comments:

Winter Menus

Comments:

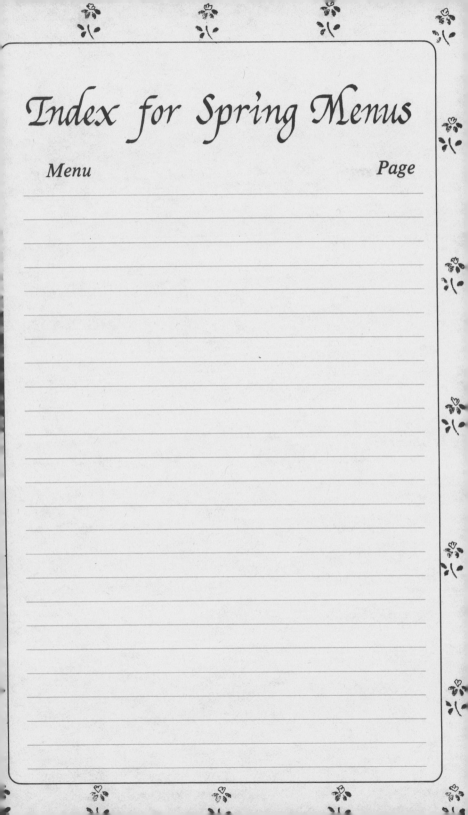

Index for Spring Menus

Menu   Page

Index

Menu	Page

Baked Ham with Fresh Asparagus

① Fresh asparagus with hollandaise

② Baked ham - could be leftover from earlier in the week. Just heat.

③ Sweet potato casserole with marshmellows on top.

④ Deviled eggs - make ahead

⑤ Rolls - from the bakery or homemade

Dessert : Either, warm rhubarb cobbler topped with ice cream (a "Yankee" dessert) or , Bananas Foster - sliced bananas cooked in butter, brown sugar, cinnamon and a dash of rum. Pour over vanilla ice cream. (a favorite Southern delight)

Comments: HINTS : Bake a large ham on Friday night for easy meals over the weekend. Ham can be served three times a day — breakfast, lunch and dinner! Cook extra asparagus and use the leftovers with the cooking liquid for a lovely cream-of-asparagus soup - reheat tomorrow.

Spring Menus

Comments:

Spring Menus

_____

_____

_____

_____

_____

_____

_____

_____

_____

_____

_____

_____

_____

_____

_____

_____

Comments:

_____

_____

_____

_____

_____

_____

Spring Menus

_____

_____

_____

_____

_____

_____

_____

_____

_____

_____

_____

_____

_____

_____

_____

_____

_____

Comments:

_____

_____

_____

_____

_____

Spring Menus

Comments:

Spring Menus

Comments:

Spring Menus

Comments:

Spring Menus

Comments:

Spring Menus

Comments:

Spring Menus

_____

_____

_____

_____

_____

_____

_____

_____

_____

_____

_____

_____

_____

_____

_____

_____

Comments:

_____

_____

_____

Spring Menus

Comments:

Spring Menus

Comments:

Spring Menus

Comments:

Spring Menus

Comments:

Spring Menus

_____
_____
_____
_____
_____
_____
_____
_____
_____
_____
_____
_____
_____
_____
_____
_____
_____

Comments:

_____
_____
_____
_____
_____
_____

Spring Menus

Comments:

Spring Menus

Comments:

Spring Menus

Comments:

Spring Menus

_____

_____

_____

_____

_____

_____

_____

_____

_____

_____

_____

_____

_____

_____

_____

_____

_____

_____

_____

Comments:

_____

_____

_____

_____

_____

Spring Menus

_____

_____

_____

_____

_____

_____

_____

_____

_____

_____

_____

_____

_____

_____

_____

_____

_____

Comments:

_____

_____

_____

_____

_____

_____

Spring Menus

_____

_____

_____

_____

_____

_____

_____

_____

_____

_____

_____

_____

_____

_____

_____

_____

_____

Comments:

_____

_____

_____

_____

_____

_____

_____

Spring Menus

_____

_____

_____

_____

_____

_____

_____

_____

_____

_____

_____

_____

_____

_____

_____

_____

_____

Comments:

_____

_____

_____

_____

_____

Comments:

Spring Menus

_____

Comments:

Comments:

Spring Menus

Comments:

Spring Menus

_____

_____

_____

_____

_____

_____

_____

_____

_____

_____

_____

_____

_____

_____

_____

_____

_____

_____

_____

_____

Comments:

_____

_____

_____

_____

_____

_____

Spring Menus

Comments:

Comments:

Spring Menus

_____

_____

_____

_____

_____

_____

_____

_____

_____

_____

_____

_____

_____

_____

_____

_____

_____

_____

_____

_____

_____

_____

Comments:

_____

_____

_____

_____

_____

_____

_____

Index for Summer Menus

Menu	Page

Index

Menu	Page

Fajitas - Mexican (Fa-hē´-tas)
cook outside on grill

We discovered this wonderful Mexican menu on a trip to Dallas, Texas. Everyone prepares his own fajita, fun and messy. Our whole family loves this meal! (They'll even help me!!)

Thin sliced beef or chicken that's been marinaded and cooked on the grill

Big flour tortillas - warmed

Guacamole - made from avocados fresh or purchase from the store

A Mexican flavored sauce - picanté, salsa, or chunky taco sauce

Sour cream, chopped lettuce, diced tomato, grated cheese

Comments: How to assemble:

Put tortilla on your plate, top with meat, sauces, vegetables. Fold — sides in, bottom up.

Have lots of iced tea ready.

Summer Menus

Comments:

Comments:

Summary Menus

Comments:

Comments:

Summer Menus

_____
_____
_____
_____
_____
_____
_____
_____
_____
_____
_____
_____
_____
_____
_____
_____
_____
_____

Comments:

_____
_____
_____
_____
_____
_____

Summer Menus

Comments:

Summer Menus

_____
_____
_____
_____
_____
_____
_____
_____
_____
_____
_____
_____
_____
_____
_____
_____
_____
_____

Comments:

_____
_____
_____
_____
_____

Comments:

Summer Menus

Comments:

Summer Menus

_____

Comments:

Summary Menus

Comments:

Summer Menus

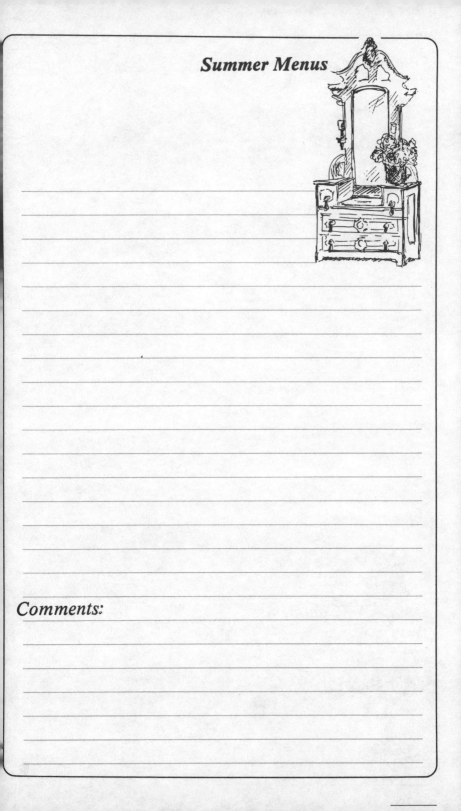

Comments:

Summer Menus

Comments:

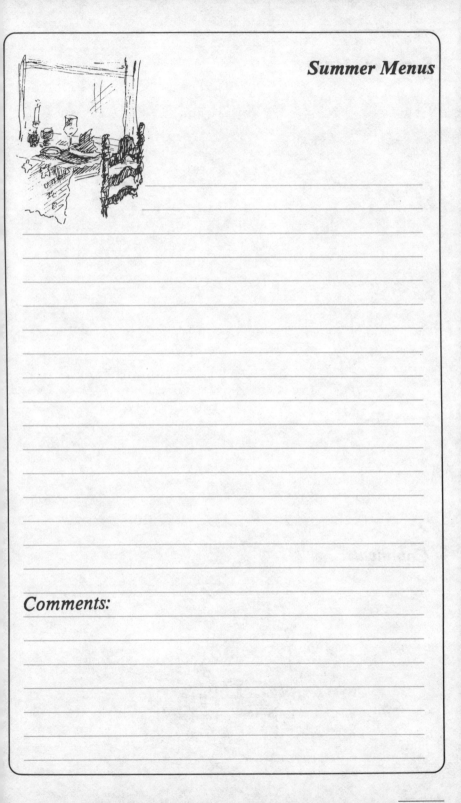

Summer Menus

Comments:

Summer Menus

Comments:

Summer Menus

_____

_____

_____

_____

_____

_____

_____

_____

_____

_____

_____

_____

_____

_____

_____

_____

_____

_____

Comments:

_____

_____

_____

_____

_____

Summer Menus

Comments:

Summer Menus

_____
_____
_____
_____
_____
_____
_____
_____
_____
_____
_____
_____
_____
_____
_____
_____
_____
_____

Comments:

_____
_____
_____
_____
_____
_____

Summer Menus

Comments:

Comments:

Summer Menus

_____

Comments:

Summer Menus

Comments:

Summer Menus

Comments:

Summer Menus

_____

_____

_____

_____

_____

_____

_____

_____

_____

_____

_____

_____

_____

_____

_____

_____

_____

_____

Comments:

_____

_____

_____

_____

_____

_____

Summer Menus

Comments:

Summer Menus

Comments:

Summer Menus

Comments:

Summer Menus

_____
_____
_____
_____
_____
_____
_____
_____
_____
_____
_____
_____
_____
_____
_____
_____
_____

Comments:
_____
_____
_____
_____
_____
_____
_____

Summer Menus

Comments:

Index for Fall Menus

Menu   **Page**

Index

Turkey and Corn Bread Dressing

Roast Turkey — 15 min. per lb. 325°

Southern Corn Bread Dressing

Gravy — make while "someone else" carves the turkey

Cranberry sauce — canned or homemade — (fresh cranberries and orange peel chopped in food processor add sugar to taste)

Fresh Brussel sprouts — prepared the Julia Child way.

Raw Carrots and Celery

Dessert: Ambrosia, a mixture of oranges, bananas, pineapple and coconut.

Comments: Make corn bread a day or two ahead & enjoy as a bread with meals. The leftover corn bread can be added to the traditional bread dressing.

Don't make ambrosia too far ahead because the bananas get brown.

Fall Menus

_____
_____
_____
_____
_____
_____
_____
_____
_____
_____
_____
_____
_____
_____
_____
_____
_____
_____

Comments:

_____
_____
_____
_____
_____
_____

Fall Menus

Comments:

Fall Menus

_____

_____

_____

_____

_____

_____

_____

_____

_____

_____

_____

_____

_____

_____

_____

_____

_____

_____

Comments:

_____

_____

_____

_____

_____

Fall Menus

_____
_____
_____
_____
_____
_____
_____
_____
_____
_____
_____
_____
_____
_____
_____
_____
_____
_____
_____

Comments:

_____
_____
_____
_____
_____
_____

Fall Menus

_____
_____
_____
_____
_____
_____
_____
_____
_____
_____
_____
_____
_____
_____
_____
_____
_____
_____
_____

Comments:

Fall Menus

Comments:

Fall Menus

_____
_____
_____
_____
_____
_____
_____
_____
_____
_____
_____
_____
_____
_____
_____
_____
_____
_____
_____

Comments:

_____
_____
_____
_____
_____
_____

Comments:

Fall Menus

_____

Comments:

Comments:

Fall Menus

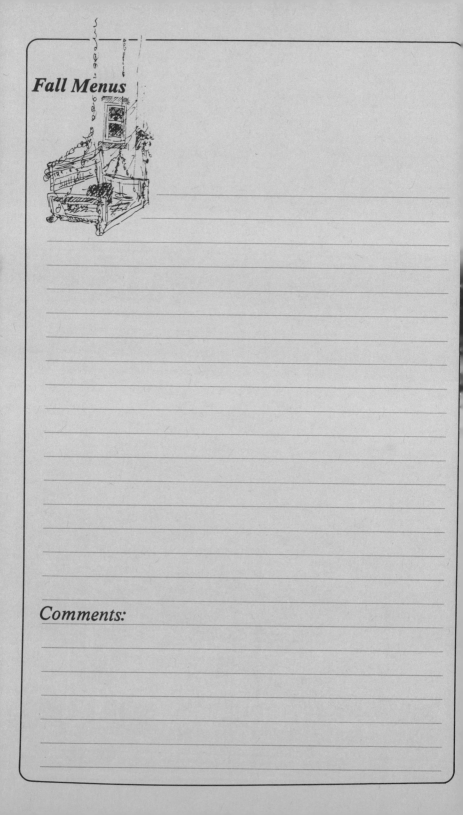

Comments:

Fall Menus

Comments:

Fall Menus

_____

_____

_____

_____

_____

_____

_____

_____

_____

_____

_____

_____

_____

_____

_____

_____

Comments:

_____

_____

_____

_____

_____

Fall Menus

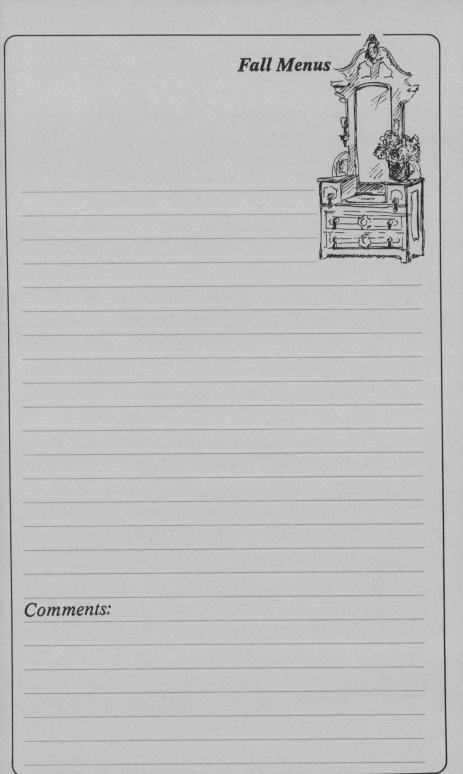

Comments:

Fall Menus

_____
_____
_____
_____
_____
_____
_____
_____
_____
_____
_____
_____
_____
_____
_____

Comments:

_____
_____
_____
_____
_____
_____

Comments:

Fall Menus

Comments:

Comments:

Fall Menus

Comments:

Fall Menus

Comments:

Fall Menus

Comments:

Fall Menus

Comments:

Fall Menus

_____

_____

_____

_____

_____

_____

_____

_____

_____

_____

_____

_____

_____

_____

_____

_____

_____

Comments:

_____

_____

_____

_____

_____

_____

_____

_____

_____

_____

_____

_____

_____

_____

_____

_____

_____

_____

_____

_____

_____

_____

Comments: _____

_____

_____

_____

_____

_____

Fall Menus

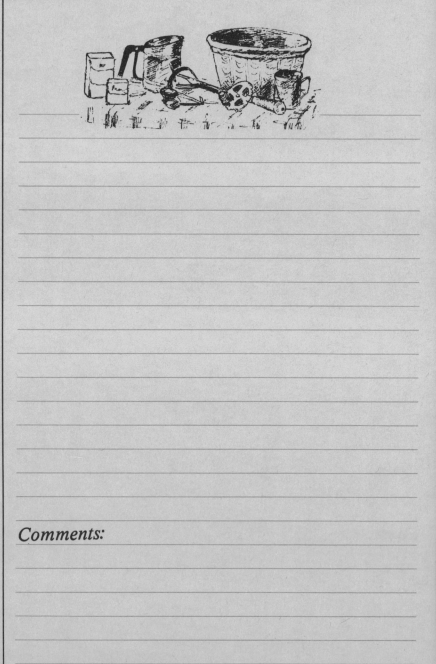

Comments:

Fall Menus

Comments:

Fall Menus

_____
_____
_____
_____
_____
_____
_____
_____
_____
_____
_____
_____
_____
_____
_____
_____
_____
_____

Comments:
_____
_____
_____
_____
_____

Comments:

Fall Menus

Comments: